# Webinar
# School

*Planning, producing, and
presenting your training webinar*

Elizabeth Frick

# Webinar School

*Planning, producing, and presenting your training webinar*

Copyright © 2016 Elizabeth Frick

## Disclaimer

The information in this book is provided on an "as is" basis, without warranty. While every effort has been taken by the author and XML Press in the preparation of this book, the author and XML Press shall have neither liability nor responsibility to any person or entity with respect to any loss or damages arising from the information contained herein.

This book contains links to third-party web sites that are not under the control of the author or XML Press. The author and XML Press are not responsible for the content of any linked site. Inclusion of a link in this book does not imply that the author or XML Press endorses or accepts any responsibility for the content of that third-party site.

## Credits

| | |
|---|---|
| Editor: | Liz Willis |
| Cover design: | Jennifer Neale Davis |
| Photo Credits: | See Appendix C (p. 63) |

## Trademarks

XML Press and the XML Press logo are trademarks of XML Press.

Webinar School and The Text Doctor are trademarks of Elizabeth Frick.

All terms mentioned in this book that are known to be trademarks or service marks have been capitalized as appropriate. Use of a term in this book should not be regarded as affecting the validity of any trademark or service mark.

XML Press
Laguna Hills, California
http://xmlpress.net

First Edition
ISBN: 978-1-937434-50-2 (print)
ISBN: 978-1-937434-51-9 (ebook)

# Table of Contents

# Acknowledgments

I try to start every day by listing gratitudes for my abundant life, so let me start this book the same way – with gratitude to those who made these pages possible:

Jane MacKenzie of Training Consultants of Sedona, who taught me everything I know about delivering webinars and who has offered excellent comments on my drafts. Jane has also graciously agreed to allow me to modify her early draft of her *Webinar Preparation and Production Checklist for Teams,* which you can find in Appendix B and in printable form on my Webliography page.[1]

Richard Hamilton of XML Press, my publisher, who has patiently guided me through the publishing of my two books. If it weren't for Richard, I'd still be stumbling around trying to figure out what to do with my first book, *Business Matters*[4].

Liz Willis, my faithful and patient editor, for her excellent developmental comments and eagle-eye copyediting.

Jen Davis of Davis Creative, Inc., for her superb graphic design skills and her beautiful cover for the book.

LisaMarie Dias of LisaMarie Designs, who offered her webinar delivery experience and comments on an early draft of the book.

Carol Davidson, AICI CIP, of StyleWorks, who is a newcomer to webinars and thus provided excellent insights about newcomers' needs.

---

[1] http://www.textdoctor.com/webinar-school-webliography/

# Preface

I have been a teacher and trainer almost all my adult life. When I was 20, I taught in a highly volatile inner city middle school, where I first learned to assess my students' body language and demeanor and adapt appropriately to each person. These skills served me well as I moved on to teach in high schools, prisons, college classrooms, corporations, and governments. I could never have imagined teaching without seeing my students – I thought I needed eye contact with them to keep my energy up.

Nine years ago, weary of my unsustainable travel schedule to deliver training, I taught my first webinar. I was determined to survive those first difficult webinars because I really, really needed to stop traveling for my training business. I had family obligations; I loved my new home in Colorado; and I believed that all those airport scanners were dangerous (I still do). So I was motivated to make webinars work for me.

Since then, I have gradually adapted to the lack of physical feedback in webinars, mostly by visualizing my students and bringing my live classroom tactics into the webinar platform. Although I longed for a book like this to help me improve my webinar delivery, most published books about webinars focus on delivering large marketing webinars (you'll see several in my Webinar School Webliography[1] and in this book's bibliography). You know that kind of webinar: hundreds, if not thousands, attend, anonymously and all muted, while presenters push out propaganda about their product or service. I have no problem with those webinars – I have attended several that were useful, but I knew that I wanted to teach in a more collegial, interactive environment.

I wrote this book for other trainers who might want to learn the best practices for producing interactive and fun webinars. How can you transfer your high engagement in the live classroom to a digital medium? I believe my experiences can help you.

---

[1] http://www.textdoctor.com/webinar-school-webliography/

## How I moved ahead

To learn more about delivering webinars, I apprenticed myself to my friend Jane MacKenzie of Training Consultants of Sedona. An excellent instructional designer and webinar producer, Jane was willing to show me how to produce her webinars in return for my taking over some production[2] roles in her webinars.

## What will you find in this book?

I love this opportunity to share what I have learned about delivering interactive, engaging webinars to help you move seamlessly into webinar delivery. I hope that any reader who might be tentative or nervous about producing webinars will find motivation and information on how to create processes for producing great webinars. We'll look at planning, preparing, producing, and presenting webinars, and I'll offer many practical tips to enhance your successful transition.

This book is exclusively about training webinars, which many trainers limit to no more than 25 participants so as to better manage their interactions. I will not cover promotional or informational webinars, usually highly produced affairs delivered to large audiences (up to 1000+ viewers).

Instead, my goal is to help you use the best features of your webinar platform to deliver your best possible training webinars. This book is purposely software agnostic so that you'll be able to translate its suggestions to whatever webinar application you choose.

I will mention two checklists often:

- Checklist A: *Checklist for webinar trainers*
- Checklist B: *Checklist for webinar teams*

---

[2] Here and elsewhere, I use the words *produce* and *production* to mean the technological act of using hardware and applications to deliver a presentation to a dispersed audience. Producing usually involves using an application to set up the webinar, managing registration and payment, delivering visual and audio input from presenter to audience, overseeing input from audience to presenter, recording the webinar, and making the recording available afterwards. Some trainers produce their own webinars and present content at the same time. Some teams appoint a producer; the presenter simply presents but doesn't take control of the webinar technology.

You'll find them in Appendices A and B and also in easy-to-print versions in my Webliography.[3] Both checklists are Microsoft Word documents that you can customize to your own needs. I will periodically update the online checklists.

Finally, I won't discuss instructional design (ID) principles – I assume that you either know those or can learn ID elsewhere. I will say that one design principle that I have applied in migrating my training content to the webinar platform is to clearly define chunks of material and build interaction into each chunk, either before, during, or after a lesson (and sometimes all three). Theoretically, we do that in our live classroom materials, but it's vital in webinar delivery if you want to keep people engaged.

I invite you to interact with me if:

- You want to start a conversation about any of my points.
- You discover new and better ways to deliver webinar technology.
- You'd like to argue about something that I have written.

Thank you – please keep in touch.

Elizabeth (Bette) Frick
efrick@textdoctor.com
     http://textdoctor.com
     https://www.linkedin.com/in/textdoctor
     https://twitter.com/bettefrick

---

[3] http://www.textdoctor.com/webinar-school-webliography

# Webinar training compared to live classroom training

In this chapter, I explore how webinars may work better than live classroom training and vice versa.

## Benefits of training by webinar

- You can reach widely dispersed audiences – often international – without the costs and hassles of travel for participants or you. Corporations and organizations also find that travel is one expense that they can happily cut by deploying webinar training.

- You can divide a long training into shorter chunks and spread those sessions over several days or weeks so that participants are away from their work responsibilities for several brief periods of time rather than for a full day or more.

- You can use the same presentation software as you do in live classroom training. You'll simply deploy it within the webinar application. Although your basic material stays the same, you may need to chunk the material more explicitly to encourage interaction through polls, chats, and breakout sessions.[1]

---

[1] I don't cover the use of breakout rooms. I have never used that tool in my own training webinars because I already squeeze an 8-hour live class into 6 hours of webinar with lots of interaction. However, I can see the value of this form of interaction.

- You can record each webinar for later review. If a participant has a conflict during a given session (illness, travel, a major problem on the manufacturing floor – life happens!), he or she can stream the recording. You might also like to review the recording to capture something you said for future scripts – or maybe you need to count your "ums." Finally, bilingual participants may wish to review the recordings if you talk too fast for them to process.

- You can choose your own level of interaction. My own webinar model includes a medium level of interaction. I offer some classes in one- or two-hour interactive segments (I view them as one-offs because I do not have further scheduled interaction with participants). I also teach an extended technical writing webinar that meets for two hours three weeks apart. Participants vote in polls and ask and answer questions in chat mode; sometimes I unmute phones for them to speak. I also meet with participants one-on-one to review writing samples and help them apply the principles taught in the webinar to their own writing.

- You will find that shy people blossom when they can chat or respond to polls anonymously. My baseline for this conclusion is that I have taught engineers and scientists for 26 years. Often, when I posed a question in live classroom training, shy engineers would avoid eye contact, perhaps fearing that I would call upon them and they might embarrass themselves with a wrong answer in a room full of their peers. Now, if I pose a question in a webinar, six or eight engineers may answer privately. Instead of revealing their names, I'll say, "Here's a good comment someone made in a private chat…" Sometimes, they even tell me jokes, a practice that I fervently encourage.

- We all save calories by avoiding the donuts in the training room.

- It's just so darn nice to not have to suit up and show up 5 or 2,000 or 7,500 miles from home.

Of course, there has to be a downside to teaching webinars, right? I am a realist, so let's look at the benefits of live classroom training.

# Benefits of live classroom training

I had coffee recently with a fellow trainer who dismissed webinar training as not being possible for her: "I'm an extrovert, and I read my participants' nonverbal body language to tell me where to go next with my responses," she told me. "I need to see them and they need to see me."

I did not dispute my colleague's classic rejection of webinars – part of me (the 26-year veteran of live classroom training) agrees wholeheartedly. For example, a recent afternoon training class at a local county office produced a huge high as participants peppered me with questions and even jokes. I do admit that I miss the nonverbal communication that we get in live classes: vocal tone, facial expression, posture, gestures, and smiles all add to the experience.

If only we lived in a perfect world where all the following conditions apply all the time to all our training:

- Travel for training is pleasant, reliable (no mega-storms to ground all flights and close all roads), and inexpensive.
- All training classes involve intact work groups located centrally and available for the full training day without interruptions.
- The last two hours of every training day are filled with energetic, lively interactions.

Trainers know that these conditions are rare or nonexistent. Yet there are situations where live classroom training is more appropriate than distance learning, including webinars; here are a few examples:

- Soft-skills training that requires role-playing and face-to-face interactions. However, many trainers are able to skillfully lead role-plays in breakout rooms within their webinar application.
- Hands-on training for machinery and technology where a live trainer can help individuals improve performance on the spot.
- Intact work groups where one objective of training is to increase group energy and cohesion.

## Maximizing webinars as a training tool

Although live classroom training is not going away any time soon, neither is webinar training. Even without face-to-face interaction, webinars do not have to be boring or particularly linear – the technology exists to create lively interaction among participants and also between participants and the trainer. It's up to us as trainers to maximize the potential of webinar technology.

Perhaps not seeing participants in webinars is simply a logical extension of faceless e-mailing and texting. We have been primed for webinars by the advent of asynchronous modes of communication that provide no visual contact with the presenter – for example, recorded TED Talks – and, thus, we can more easily adapt to this mode of synchronous distance learning, especially when interactions create a bond between trainer and participant.

You may be concerned about the potential for participants to multitask (check their mobile devices, answer e-mail, send texts) and not pay attention to your slides or your words. Remember, though, that multitasking happens in live classroom training, too.

A vice president in a major medical manufacturing firm hired me to train his people to write better. To his credit, he attended the training, but he paid far more attention to his mobile device than he did to our class discussions. Of course, since he would be signing off on my invoice, I wasn't going to challenge him! The funniest thing happened, though – about five minutes after I had made a very distinct point about technical writing, he asked a question that indicated that he hadn't heard a word of what I said. Everybody's jaws dropped. So, yes, multitasking occurs in both live classroom training and webinars, but at least in webinars, we can use polls and chats to help focus our participants without directly calling them out.

So, until I can buy and staff that private jet, I'll continue to teach my Technical Writing webinars wearing my bunny slippers.

# CHAPTER 2

# Planning your webinar

Advance planning for a webinar is no more complicated than planning live classroom training and probably less if you factor out potential travel arrangements. Of course, your planning will go much smoother if you use a checklist.

Oh, yawn. Checklists are so boring, aren't they?

Think again. Here are three examples of lifesaving checklists:

1. Captain Chesley Sullenberger kept trying to restart the engines on his A320, which had been disabled by birds, while checking off emergency landing procedures on a three-page list that the crew normally begins at 35,000 feet. If I had been a passenger on this plane on January 15, 2009, I would have been very grateful that the crew had a checklist of procedures for emergency landings and was using it! (All 155 on board survived.)

2. A study published in the *New England Journal of Medicine* in January 2009 reported that doctors worldwide who followed a checklist of steps cut surgical death rates almost in half and complications by more than a third. One item on the surgical checklist was "Scrawl on the patient with a permanent marker to show where the surgeon should cut." If I were the patient, I'd welcome that permanent marker.

3. Atul Gawande's *The Checklist Manifesto: How to Get Things Right* [5] reports how implementing checklists for surgeons and nurses in Johns Hopkins Hospital over one year resulted in the 10-day line infection rate going from 11% to zero.

The stakes in planning and producing webinars may not be as high as for flight crews and surgeons, but a checklist will help any trainer manage the many technical necessities required to deliver a webinar. None of the individual production activities is difficult, but you must execute the steps in a certain order. It's the only way I know to easily keep track and execute all the activities involved.

Here are a few considerations for planning your training webinar:

- When scheduling, be mindful of time zones in the United States and throughout the world. Consider surveying participants for the best timing for them; this request has the additional benefit of establishing interaction right away.
- Schedule the webinar in your webinar application.
- Once you select a time for your webinar and invite participants to sign up or attend, consider providing a map showing the webinar start time in all the participants' time zones. Some brilliant people are time-zone challenged! Be sure to communicate the relevant time zones frequently. Here is an example for a webinar scheduled in the United States:
  - 9 AM Pacific, 10 AM Mountain, 11 AM Central, 12 noon Eastern.
- Unless you plan to produce your webinar from your own office, select and book a room or a venue in which to produce. In an office setting, you must have a lockable door, as much sound deadening as possible, and no windows if you plan to show your webcam (a windowless room reduces lighting difficulties).

You can find other planning steps in Appendix B, *Checklist for webinar teams*.

# CHAPTER 3

# Preparing content for your training webinar

**Webinar**
Web-based seminar
live online educational pre~
viewers can submit questions
see slides while the speaker
interactive elements - the a'

In this chapter, I discuss how to prepare your webinar content and spell out the steps that you need to take for optimum webinar delivery. Much of what I address here appears more briefly in Appendix A, *Checklist for webinar trainers*, which you can download and modify for your needs.

## Three weeks ahead

1. Finalize your message and your slides (see Chapter 10 for tips on creating better slides).
2. When you feel confident that your content is final, create your polls (see Chapter 7 for more information on polls). Polls can function as surveys of opinions and ideas or as mastery checks (measurement to see if the objectives were achieved). See Figure 3.1.

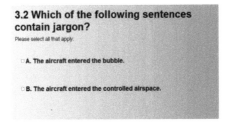

**3.2 Which of the following sentences contain jargon?**
Please select all that apply.

□ A. The aircraft entered the bubble.

□ B. The aircraft entered the controlled airspace.

Figure 3.1 – Sample mastery-check poll

3. Add introductory slides to your content to help your class understand how your webinar application functions. Here are three standard introductory slides that I reuse early in all my webinars. The first slide (Figure 3.2) is a picture of the participants' control panel, which you can use to explain how to use the panel.

Figure 3.2 – Show and explain viewers' control panel

4. The second slide (Figure 3.3) shows them how to chat.

## Please try chatting

- You'll use chat function for two purposes:
  - You can respond to my questions in "chat" fashion.
    - •Please chat now: How is my sound quality?
  - You can ask a question or tell a joke.
  - Don't worry about typos.

Figure 3.3 – Encourage participants to chat

5. The third slide (Figure 3.4) urges participants not to multitask.

**Let's agree...**

- Let's not multitask during webinar.
  – You can multitask during our 10-minute break.
- For best webinar functionality, please close all other programs.
- Please ask questions as soon as you think of them.
- Most examples taken from company documents
  – Not meant to embarrass
  – Meant to make webinar more relevant than generic examples
  – Selected randomly from many documents

Figure 3.4 – Discourage multitasking

# Two weeks ahead and up to your webinar day

6. Rehearse! Rehearse! Rehearse! Rehearse your script and slides by practicing within your application.

   a. Don't get complacent even as you become more experienced: I have used the same webinar application for nine years, but I never rest on my laurels and assume I will operate all the technology smoothly. No single, specific feature is complicated on my application, but the confluence of presenting online, watching and responding to chat, and launching polls could easily go awry if I were to trust habit completely. Post-production activities especially slip my mind. Of course, practice will make these steps more habitual and automatic so that you can focus on your message.

   b. Rehearsals are even more essential if you have multiple presenters and if you are the producer. Everyone must understand their roles and must practice using the technology.

7. Respond to any e-mail questions that participants may send before your broadcast.

8. Use e-mail to query participants if you don't know how to pronounce their names. This allows you to both establish interaction early and avoid embarrassment in the webinar; your participants will appreciate your thoughtfulness.

# CHAPTER 4

# Producing and presenting your live training webinar

Always use a procedure or checklist to guide you while producing your webinars. In this chapter, I expand and explain the procedural steps listed in my checklist for producing webinars (Appendix A, *Checklist for webinar trainers*). This discussion assumes that you (the trainer) are also producing your webinar. If you're producing your webinar with a team, you can also use the checklist in Appendix B, *Checklist for webinar teams*.

## Webinar day!

1. Log on at least a half hour early. For now, leave in place the generic slide that most webinar applications provide.

2. Connect to audio about 20 minutes before broadcast time and test your microphone or phone headset. Then MUTE yourself!

> When you mute yourself, tape or hang a note on your microphone or telephone that says, "I'm muted." When you're ready to speak again, pull off the note, unmute yourself, and start broadcasting audio again.

3. About 10 minutes before your webinar is to start, launch your first slide with the statement: "We'll get going at the top of the hour" (or whatever is appropriate for your start time). I use clip art to show the top of the hour:

4. At the start time, precisely:[1]
   a. Unmute yourself
   b. Start the webinar
5. And have fun!

Good, now you're launched. Consider these suggestions:

- If possible, stand up so that you might emulate a live classroom and keep your energy up. Consider using a stand-up desk (you can find suppliers listed in the Webliography).
- Visualize your audience. If you need to feel their presence, post a picture of a live audience on your office wall (I use Figure 4.1) and smile back at them (your participants won't **see** your smile, but they will **hear** it).
- Wave your arms. Gesture to the audience and to your screen(s) as if you were in an actual classroom.

---

[1] Why start precisely on time? I hate when webinar or classroom trainers say, "I'll start the class in a few minutes to make sure everyone is here. Thank you for your patience." I am most certainly not patient waiting for others to show up after start time. What a poor way to train participants that they can be late for class and waste valuable webinar time! Along the same lines, always finish right on time as well.

Figure 4.1 – I like to visualize my participants using this image[2]

One final suggestion: No matter how many years' experience you've had as a trainer, if you have not joined Toastmasters[3] and completed the first 10 speeches, please join as soon as you can and learn everything they can teach you. Toastmasters provides amazing help in delivering all types of live presentations and will develop your skills at a very reasonable price. You will learn how to overcome any reluctance or fear of presenting in front of people, and that will help you with any nervousness in presenting webinars.

---

[2] Image licensed from IStock.

[3] http://www.toastmasters.org/

# CHAPTER 5

# After your webinar

You have closed out your webinar (precisely on time) and thanked the participants profusely for their interactions and engagement. Now, a lot of post-webinar work lies ahead, but at least there's less pressure than when preparing for or producing your webinar.

## Perform post-webinar activities

Immediately after you close your webinar, you may be tempted to leave your office to celebrate. However, before you do that, complete these activities:

- Upload the recording to storage and send the link to the recording to attendees (if sharing with them).
- Download the attendance reports and store in folder.
- Download the chat log.
- Unmute/unsilence devices that you muted earlier.

Of course, how you perform these activities will vary from platform to platform. The *Checklist for webinar trainers* in Appendix A provides a quick overview of how to close out your webinar.

## Mine the chat log

After each webinar, I mine the chat log for opportunities to interact further with participants individually, perhaps by answering a question that we didn't have time to discuss in the webinar; expanding on an answer to a question during the webinar; or commenting on a great point that a participant made.

I love having the chat log as a permanent record of the class comments. Unlike a live classroom, where interaction just keeps washing over me without my being able to capture it, the chat log is a priceless tool that allows me to capture the most brilliant statements and answers and add those to the Notes section of relevant slides for future use (read more about chatting in Chapters 7 and 8). Chat logs are also a great source of content and prompts for future webinars as well as questions that you can answer in a blog post or article.

## Capture lessons learned

Be sure to spend a moment on one final activity: as suggested in Appendix A, *Checklist for webinar trainers*, jot down "lessons learned" and briefly list what went well and what you'll do better in your next webinar.

# CHAPTER 6

# Low-tech tips for interactivity

Up to this point, I haven't focused on how you can make your webinars interactive and engaging. In this chapter, I talk about low-tech tips for personal interactivity – techniques that engage participants but don't require technical tools within your webinar application. Think of these as interactions that you may already initiate in live classroom training. If you are transitioning to delivering training by webinar, you'll see how you can transfer those activities into your webinar classrooms. In Chapter 7, I explore the glorious technology that supports creative, compelling interactivity with your participants.

Many trainers believe, as I once did, that interactivity in our live classroom training comes from a two-way visual and auditory connection with the participant – that we get energy from our participants and vice versa. It wasn't until I started teaching webinars that I understood that even if I didn't see them and they didn't see me, my participants and I could still connect in a meaningful way.

Low-tech interactivity is generally non-digital and may allow for a different type of connection – it helps a trainer engage individual participants in personal ways that make them feel that the trainer has paid attention to them, individually and collectively.

Here's one way that I create this type of engagement in my live classroom: When I am setting up my room and the first participants come in early, I shake their hands and joke around with them as they settle in.

As more participants come in and fill out their name tents, I walk up to those whose names might challenge me and quietly ask them how to pronounce their names. Then I say the name a few times and verify that I have it right.

If, by chance, I have a participant with the same name as a family member or a good friend (or even my name), I'll tease, "Bruce, you'll get an A for the class!" When asked why, I'll say that my first-born son is named Bruce. Of course, it's a non-graded course, and everyone knows that. But I like to think that these jokes start the class off right.

## Address webinar participants

At the beginning of a webinar, I mention that we have participants "from California, Minnesota, New Jersey, Puerto Rico, and Switzerland." Just as in live classroom training, I try to address webinar participants by first name as often as I can. Here is an example: "Yolanda, I like this comment in your chat about acronyms: 'Another problem with acronyms is when they need to be translated to a different language – if there isn't a glossary, it can be impossible for the translator to know what they mean and how to translate them.'" People love the sound of their own name and the simple act of dropping a participant's name into a sentence creates awareness in the group of participants that you recognize all of them as individuals.

Of course, just as in live classes, there will always be names that present pronunciation challenges (for example, Abdulhafez, Soniya, Zhiman, Katarzyna, or Aisling). I send e-mail to these participants before our webinar series to ask how they pronounce their names and explain that I don't want to embarrass either of us by saying their name wrong. They always thank me for taking the time to check on this.

I particularly enjoy chatting with students in those last minutes before the webinar starts promptly at the top of the hour. Here's the chat log of a private chat with a participant in Ireland (with whom I had already established a relationship because he shares a name with my youngest son):

> **Elizabeth Frick (to Daniel): 9:53 AM:** Hi, Daniel! How are you today?
> **Daniel (to Organizer(s) Only): 9:55 AM:** I am fine Bette. Trust all is well at your side.
> **Elizabeth Frick (to Daniel): 9:56 AM:** Yup, thank you for asking. We have about 10 inches of snow and more on the way. It is beautiful! So Christmasy (oops, that's not a word. Don't tell anyone in the class :-)
> **Daniel (to Organizer(s) Only): 9:58 AM:** :-)

I talk more about chatting in Chapter 7.

## Encourage peer feedback

A powerful, low-tech interaction that I use in the third of our three Technical Writing webinars is to gain permission from a participant to show a small sample document for class feedback. Again, because many of my engineers are shy, I offer a bribe (er, incentive) in the form of a gift card to the vendor of their choice. I have never had trouble getting a volunteer!

I then tell my class that we will exercise their feedback muscles by allowing them to comment on their peer's sample document. I use the slide in Figure 6.1 to prompt them to structure their comments using "I like" and "I wish" statements.

### Giving and receiving feedback

- First: Share "I like" statements
  - I like your graphic on page 2.
  - I like your sentence structure in the 3rd paragraph.
  - I like your explanation of _____ .
- Then: Share "I wish" statements
  - I wish that you had presented this paragraph in a table.
  - How about providing a summary at the beginning that lets me know what this e-mail is about?
  - How about including a picture of this process so I could visualize it better?
- Or even "consider" statements
  - Consider moving this paragraph up to the beginning.

Figure 6.1 – Explaining feedback techniques

As we begin this activity, I unmute the author of the document so that he or she can provide us with the context for the document, and then I sit back and watch the intense chatting while the author responds out loud to questions and comments. The peer comments are usually so helpful that I e-mail that portion of the chat log to the author.

# Inject humor where you can

Humor can aid your interactions and create more fun for everyone. I use humor mainly to keep myself amused in spite of the lack of visual feedback from a remote audience. Here are some funny words that I use throughout my slides:

- **Voluntold:**   "Perhaps you were voluntold to take this class?"
- **Administrivia:**   I use this made-up word as the title of my slide about administrative details.
- **Automagically:**   I use this where appropriate.

I have had participants chat LOL or e-mail me after class to ask if that was a *real* word? At the very least, I know they were paying attention.

I keep surprising participants with a constant stream of random but relevant funny pictures and jokes. (I stole this tactic from a Delta Airlines onboarding video that was so hilarious, I watched to the end – a first for me.) Most of my webinar humor relates to language and technical writing, of course. Some of my pictures were sent by former participants, which I mention.

On the last slide of my Technical Writing webinar series, I show a picture of a graduating class of beautiful young people (Figure 6.2) and play a re-cording of *Pomp and Circumstance* as I congratulate my participants for completing the course. I always get a good reaction from my participants – including LOLs – at this admittedly corny ploy.

Figure 6.2 – Our virtual graduation ceremony

# Bring in something of interest from participants' documents

Another way to engage participants is to acknowledge something that they have said or written. For example, in my technical writing webinar, I can easily find some cool words that I have never seen before in participants' writing samples, and I share these words at the beginning of the final session. I include these words on an introductory slide that shows onscreen while we are waiting for the webinar to begin:

Best new words of the webinar series:
**Cavitation:** The pitting and wearing away of solid surfaces [to create a cavity, I guess] (thank you, Nick!)
**Skive:** To cut thin layers or pieces (thank you, Daniel!)

## Interact after the webinar

**Encourage them to keep in touch:**    At the end of our last webinar, I always encourage my participants to keep in touch with questions or to send me jokes – and some do both!

**Mine the chat log:**    As I mentioned in Chapter 5, after each webinar, I comb the chat log to look for opportunities to contact students. I might write to George and expand on my answer to his question – perhaps I have thought of additional information or I might even reverse my original answer. If Claudia offered a brilliant example of tightening a wordy sentence, I might send e-mail to praise her for her excellent answer. We might be communicating as faceless entities, but we now have positive interactions to bond us. And if there are students who seem particularly willing to connect, I ask them to connect with me on LinkedIn. I might also mention that I have X number of contacts in their organization; many participants, especially new hires, would love to have this sort of exposure.

All of these low-tech tips for encouraging interaction should remind you of what you do in your live classroom training session; I hope that you will realize that in webinars, just as in your classroom, you can use your personality and empathy to reach out and connect with your participants – for their benefit and yours!

That being said, I need to acknowledge that live classroom training probably does offer unique opportunities for low-tech interactivity that would be difficult to pull off with a webinar. For example, I doubt that any webinar will ever be able to recreate the funniest thing that ever happened to me in my training career. Remember my son Bruce? I used that joke to "reward" a man named Bruce as I kicked off a Technical Writing class at Smead Manufacturing (Hastings, Minnesota). Imagine my surprise when, after writing some extended text on a flip chart, I turned around and everyone's name tent said "Bruce." I loved that they were playing back the joke on me.

# CHAPTER 7

# High-tech tips for interactivity

Chapter 6 explored low-tech ways to establish a relationship with individual participants and with the class as a whole – where possible – to enhance engagement when you don't see them and they don't see you. This chapter explores high-tech (digital) interactions within your webinar application that you can initiate with the whole class.

Most higher-end webinar applications provide chatting, polling, webcams, open audio lines, and testing capabilities to enhance interactivity. My application lets me share my keyboard and mouse controls with a participant, saying, "Here: You drive!" Many applications allow you to share videos, write on a whiteboard, share webcams, and display profile pictures in chats.

In this chapter, I discuss how to explain webinar tools to participants, encourage chatting, produce polls, share webcams, deliver tests, and employ other interactions that are effective and fun.

## Explain your application

Early in your introductory slides, include a slide that shows the participants' control panel. I provide a visual of the control panel with callouts to main features (see Chapter 3) to show them tips like these:

- How to expand and collapse the control panel
- How to unclick "Autohide the control panel" so they can follow the chat
- How to chat publicly (Entire Audience) or privately to the presenter only

Make sure that they understand the application before you move on.

I always tell my participants, "For best results, close other programs running on your desktop," and I explain that our application requires a lot of bandwidth and may even crash or close if competing with too many other applications. I'm not exactly sure that this is true, but I hope that it discourages them from multitasking too much.

## Show them how to chat

I tell participants: "You are muted so that we can minimize background noise and Voice Over Internet Protocol (VOIP) interference. You can ask me to unmute you at any time if you would like to ask a question." I go on to say the following:

- Use the chat window to type your questions or comments.
- Please chat now: How is my sound quality? Too loud, too soft, just right?
- Please note that you can chat privately or anonymously to me – I'm listed in your chat window as Private, Organizer, or Presenter. If you chat privately, I won't mention your name if I read your comments.
- You can also use the chat function to send me jokes – please do!

In a webinar with a small group of participants (say, 10 or fewer), you might consider offering a small incentive for the participant who chats the most – it's amazing how competition for a $10 Starbucks card can drive those chatting fingers! But in a larger group, you will probably have more chat than you can respond to during the webinar.

I schedule a chat opportunity or a poll (discussed in the next section) at least every 5 to 7 minutes to encourage participation and interaction (and maybe interrupt their multitasking). For example, I may ask the class to revise a sentence to half its original length, or ask them to place punctuation in a sentence to make it more readable.

# Practice polling

I try to deliver 4 to 5 polls per hour. I remind all participants that poll results are aggregated and anonymous, so they do not have to worry about being embarrassed by any mistakes that they might make. I print out the poll questions and answers for my own reference.

In my introduction, I show a sample poll slide (see Figure 7.1 ) and run a sample poll so they can practice this form of interactivity.

### Poll 1: Poll on webinars

Please choose the appropriate response from the list provided in the poll.

Responses are aggregated; yours will be completely anonymous.

Figure 7.1 – Sample polling slide

Figures 7.2 and 7.3 show a sample poll question and the results.

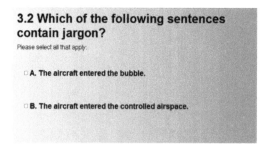

Figure 7.2 – Poll question as participants see it

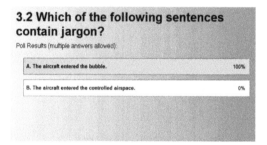

Figure 7.3 – Poll results as participants see them

To avoid making technical mistakes during polling, consider faithfully following a script like this to walk yourself through each step of producing a successful poll:

1. OK, now I'm going to launch our next poll.
2. This poll asks you to _____.
3. Oh, I like how diverse your answers are!
4. We're at 90%, shooting for 100% of you to take the poll.
5. OK, I'll close the poll and share the results with you. [Share results and discuss]
6. Thanks for taking the poll; I'll close the results and return to the slides.

If I don't follow a script like this, I inevitably leave the poll up on their screen and launch into the rest of my slides on my own screen. Participants soon let me know, but it's embarrassing!

I announce the last poll of the webinar: "This is our last poll, folks. Thanks so much for all your participation in the polls!"

## Use webcams

Webcams are a high-tech tool that might help you personalize your webinar. However, showing your webcam or having them show theirs throughout the webinar requires a lot of bandwidth, so you might want to use this option only briefly.

Another downside to using webcams is that you need to tidy your office or use a screen behind you. I use a three-panel screen to hide pictures, books, and objects behind me in the office, although I do realize that those items would make the background more personal and realistic.

Sometimes I show my webcam at the beginning of the webinar and urge them to show theirs if they wish. I'll explain about the bandwidth issue and gracefully wave goodbye. I definitely try to use my webcam when I meet one-on-one with participants for our coaching sessions. I find that my shy engineers tend not to show their own webcams, in which case I stop showing mine because of any power differential that the webcam might create between us.

## Open audio lines

In my webinar introduction, I explain that all participants are muted to avoid background noise or VOIP interference. I also tell them that I would be delighted to open their audio line to allow them to offer a question, a comment, or a rant. Again, engineers and technical employees seem to loathe the spotlight and rarely ask for this option.

I have attended large marketing webinars where presenters will unmute participants in the audience randomly, without warning, and ask them to speak. I've even been on the receiving end of that experience – and I don't recommend it. I'd rather unmute willing students who choose to speak.

## Launch tests

Many applications allow you to launch a test before, during, or after a webinar. You can usually choose to let participants see the answers after they complete the test, or you can discuss the answers in the webinar after all have completed the test.

Due to time constraints, I usually do not launch tests during the webinar, but I do offer a voluntary post-test and provide the answers after they complete the test. Figure 7.4 shows a screenshot of a sample online post-test in GoToTraining.

### Webinar VOLUNTARY Post-test

Close Instructions

Please test your learning after the webinar. Let me know if you have any questions!

Thank you.

Bette Frick
efrick@textdoctor.com

1. **Best practices for prewriting include (Select all that apply.)**
   - [ ] a. Prewrite in your head rather than on paper as it will save you time.
   - [ ] b. Write down whatever pops into your head. Don't censor anything at this point--just write it down. You can delete it later.
   - [ ] c. Use clustering, mindmapping, and/or brainstorming tools to access your right hemisphere.
   - [ ] d. Skip prewriting altogether to save yourself time.

2. **Most adults in western cultures use their _____ (brain) hemisphere predominantly.**
   - ○ a. Right
   - ○ b. Left

Figure 7.4 – Sample online post-test

## Interact in other ways

- You can hand over your keyboard and mouse controls to a participant, saying, "Here: You drive!" when it would be useful for them to modify a document or even show their own screen.

- Use drawing tools if you have them in your application; however, I am so pathetic at drawing that I resist this unless I want to provide an opportunity for them to laugh at me.

- Consider viewing your interactions from the participant's perspective by enrolling yourself in one of your webinars and watching the interactions on another computer. There's a downside to this: I find it distracting to teach and also watch the webinar on my other laptop when I am actually producing the webinar on my two screens.

Want proof that interactions work? Read these statements from my webinar evaluations:

- I really liked the chat feature – it brought out the competitive spirit in all of us.
- Participation and polls made it interesting.
- Bette used all the available tools in the environment to keep the team engaged. She made this work really well.
- Bette requires you to pay attention when you have polls and chats. I like that she asks for comments via chat so nobody can goof off or multitask.
- Chats and polls kept the attendees engaged.
- I would rather participate through polls and chats than actively participating in a classroom environment.
- [I liked] the ease of participation. Chat function works well to obtain input without interrupting presenter's flow of information.

# CHAPTER 8

# Technology tips: hardware, presentation software, audio, Internet

And now, a true confession: I do not have a smartphone – just a cheap, prepaid phone that allows me to call and text. I suffer a lot of ridicule from friends and family and am embarrassed when my nine-year-old granddaughter has to show me how to access the very few features that I have on my dumb phone (and charges me $2 for each tip). But the truth is that I've never understood the **why** of a smartphone for me.

However, I have been more than eager to learn the intricacies of webinar production and to wade through the new rollouts of improved technology in my chosen application. I have been willing to go beyond my usual level of comfort because this technology allows me to sit in my office in my bunny slippers and teach rather than travel halfway around the world to teach. I consider it a miracle that I was able to learn all the intricacies of webinar delivery. If you are adept at technology to begin with, you'll probably learn much faster!

# Hardware

Here's what I have learned about using hardware to help me produce the best webinars that I can:

## *Use two monitors if possible*

And yes, "bigger IS better" when it comes to monitors! If your only monitor is HUGE, perhaps you can position your control panel and chat window on the same screen as your slide. I love my two monitors (see Figure 8.1) because all that monitor geography allows me to see everything that's happening in my webinar.

Figure 8.1 – My monitor setup in presenter view

I run my slides on my left screen and position the production properties and presenter view on my bigger screen on the right. I undock and expand the following properties and enlarge them as much as possible:

- Chat log
- Polling tool
- Audience view

How to select presenter view in Microsoft PowerPoint (if you have two monitors).
Select: Slide Show → Use Presenter View → Show on Primary Monitor

Now you can access your script in your Notes section by viewing it on your second monitor.

## Presentation software

For me, the Notes section in presenter view is invaluable. In Chapter 5, I mentioned that I could mine prior chat logs for really good audience responses to my questions or really good comments, questions, and jokes. I copy and paste the best of the best into the Notes section for each relevant slide. Then, in those inevitable dead spots after I pose a question, when I might become nervous because no one seems to be answering, I calmly view my Notes section in presenter view and say: "Here's a private chat that says 'I had to read the second sentence three times aloud....' "

In the meantime, participants will be seeing public chats in the chat log and may be inspired to offer a chat or respond to a chat.

## Audio

When I first began producing webinars in 2006, I used a cordless phone on my landline because I could not afford anything better. Soon, I upgraded to a professional landline phone and a wireless Plantronics headset. Later, I found a Samson CO3U USB microphone that provides excellent sound quality for my webinars and one-on-one coaching sessions.

Now, when I do my mic check in my introduction and ask the participants to chat about my sound quality, the feedback is almost always: "Great!" "Just right!" "Clear." "Volume is fine." My goal is to sound as professional as I can within my budget.

Your best sound technology choices in descending order of quality:

- USB microphone
- Wireless landline headset
- Corded landline
- Mobile phone

If you want to know more about sound quality, take any webinar that you can from Robert Hershenow.[1] Everything I know about sound, I learned from Robert, and I continue to learn from him.

### To mute or not to mute

I mute everyone when I have more than five participants. Surprisingly, many people do not know how to mute their own landlines, mobile phones, or USB microphones, even when I explain the process to them. Muting everyone from my end avoids participants' background office noise and VOIP distortions that only distract everyone. I tell participants to chat to tell me that they want to speak so I can unmute them.

If you choose not to mute participants, remind them to mute themselves unless they want to speak. (My usually shy engineers do not often ask to speak, but sometimes they do!)

## Internet connection

Your Internet connection will have two speeds: download and upload. Download speed – the speed of content coming to you – is important for displaying Web pages quickly and for watching streaming video on sites such as Netflix and YouTube. However, upload speed – the speed of content going from you to your participants – is important for sending data to other computers or to your webinar application. Generally, upload speeds are much slower than download speeds because most Internet service providers cater to individual subscribers, who usually download rather than upload.

---

[1] http://rdhcommunications.com/

My upload speed of 6.09 Mbps (see Figure 8.2) is good, and I can move between slides without much delay. Of course, corporate speeds are no doubt much faster than individual subscribers' speeds.

Be sure to check your actual upload speed and compare that to your webinar application requirements for maximum audio clarity and quick transitions between slides. Aim for the highest possible upload speed to ensure smooth delivery and always prefer your local area network (LAN) to wireless because a LAN should have the highest upload speed (and of course is more secure). Figure 8.2 shows my download and upload speeds as revealed by speedtest.net.[2]

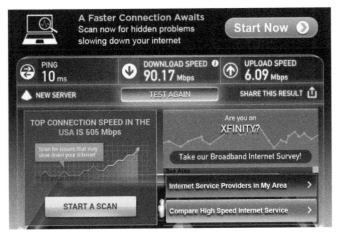

Figure 8.2 – My download and upload speeds

Avoid using a mobile phone as your primary sound system unless you are forced to do so because your landline or VOIP connection fails. Mobile phone quality is just too unreliable.

Consider diversifying technology suppliers. Avoid using just one megacompany for Internet, telephone, and mobile phone service. Outages happen, but having diverse suppliers means that you can plan wisely how you might avoid potential surprises (I will discuss surprises in Chapter 9).

---

[2] http://www.speedtest.net/

# CHAPTER 9
# Expect three surprises!

With so much technology to manage, always expect surprises in your webinar. If you anticipate these inevitable surprises rather than fear them, you are more likely to perform under pressure rather than become rattled.

I learned this valuable life principle years ago when I volunteered to work with a team rebuilding an orphanage in Jamaica. Our trainer stressed: "Expect three surprises!" That was certainly true in a third-world country:

- Our biggest truck got stuck in the muddy mess of dirt roads halfway up a mountain in monsoon season.
- Our shipment of materials never showed up.
- I fell in love with Edward, an 8-year-old orphan with cerebral palsy. (Surprises can be good, I have learned!)

Since then, I have applied the principle of expecting three surprises in my personal and professional life. In any given day, I may encounter one or three or nine surprises, but the point is – I expect surprises, and that makes it easier to deal with them. Sometimes, the technology surprises me, and sometimes I suffer from operator error.

Here are a few of the many surprises (some self-inflicted) that I have experienced while producing webinars (fortunately, not all at once):

- I forgot to add a last-minute poll to my system.

- I left the poll results on my screen as I launched into my next slide; the participants were left viewing the poll results instead of the slides.

- I muted myself for a break and forgot to unmute myself.

- My webinar application was upgraded overnight – with no warning – and I didn't have time to explore or learn the new and enhanced production properties before I had to start broadcasting.

- My ISP had an outage that started 30 minutes before I began producing, and I had to cancel the webinar.

Expecting surprises means that rather than panicking or crumbling when something unforeseen happens, you acknowledge it, fix it, and move on.

Just be sure to add the fix to your checklist so you won't make the same mistake again or panic if the problem is out of your control. For example, if you tend to forget to unmute yourself, add this: "Post a sticky note that says 'I am muted' over mic [phone] when I mute myself. Take sticky note off after I unmute myself."

## Hardware backup: plan redundant technology

You may not have control over all your technology issues, but if you do, there are some specific steps that you can take. Most involve having redundant technology in case one system fails. An aircraft cockpit (see Figure 9.1) provides a classic example of redundant technology.

Figure 9.1 – Redundancy in the cockpit

- Maintain a backup computer/laptop with your webinar software installed.
- Keep an extra mouse on hand.
- Update your operating system and webinar software frequently on all your computers/laptops.
- If possible, connect your backup laptop to your LAN rather than trust wireless.
- Have your mobile phone handy in case other audio options fail.
- Always have support numbers and URLs for your Internet provider, your webinar software provider, and anyone else you might need to call in an emergency.
- Back up your webinar recordings onto DVDs or an external hard drive and keep them in a secure place.

# CHAPTER 10

# How not to kill your webinar with your slides

Most of our discussion so far has focused on becoming a confident webinar producer/trainer. But how good are your presentation slides?

Many books will help you design and create better slides; this chapter will merely touch the surface of improving your webinars by improving your slides. Let's look at five content and five visual principles to make your slides more attractive, compelling, and professional.

## Five content principles for better slides

1. **Create a story:** At least, tell your audience **what, so what,** and **now what** – the basic blueprint for telling stories. For example, when I present my webinar *Writing More Effective Proposals,* I demonstrate the story technique by telling how a former employee swiped a credit card instead of an employee badge to enter the clean room (that's the **what** – the facts), how this could have affected a concurrent security audit (that's the **so what**), and how I recommended a new security system to fix the problem (that's the **now what**).

2. **Organize your thoughts:** Use any method of clustering, mind mapping, brainstorming – any non-linear technique that allows you to access your right hemisphere – to find the organization inherent in your random thoughts about your story.

3. **Show your organization:** Use your slide hierarchy to show levels of organization both within the slides and between slides. Make sure that at every point in your slide show, you are making the structure of your presentation completely clear to your participants so they feel more comfortable about your message.

4. **Use ≤ six words in your bullet points:** You must become a wizard at tightening slide text to meet this goal. "But," you say, "there's so much information that I need to put on the slide." If you plan to fill each slide with 100 or more words, you can expect that most webinar participants will be multitasking and not even looking at your slides. However, if you prioritize keywords over sentences, those keywords will prompt you to say everything that you need to say about that point – and keep your audience from zoning out.

5. **Use simple words where appropriate:** I know, I know – you need to establish your credibility as an expert in your field and most technical words are mul-ti-syl-lab-ic. But technical readers will welcome a few shorter, Saxon words to balance those long, Latinate words. For example, the Latinate word "u-til-ize" rarely carries more information or meaning than the Saxon word "use." Wherever you can, use the shortest words possible to express your ideas, especially on screen.

## Five visual principles for better slides

1. **Select a simple, professional template:** You may be confined to using your corporate templates. If not, know that the templates in Microsoft PowerPoint have improved greatly over the years, but they can still be way too busy. You are probably better off starting with a blank template and creating your own design, perhaps by copying designs that you really like. Aim for the utmost simplicity.

2. **Use sans serif typefaces:** Serif typefaces have strokes or lines on the letters; sans serif typefaces do not. (I think of san serif as the IKEA of typefaces: very clean lines with no frills.) Sans serif works best on-screen, especially for slides, partly because serif typefaces tend to pixelate when enlarged. Microsoft sans serif defaults (Verdana, Tahoma, and Calibri) have adequate spacing between letters and make attractive

onscreen typefaces. Don't use Arial or Arial Narrow in slides because there is just too little space between letters to allow optimum readability. Save those tight sans serif typefaces for cells in tables, callouts, titles – wherever you need to fit a lot of text into a tight space.

3. **Show the idea:** Here is where pictures, graphics, and tables are your best friends. Show, don't tell; or at least, tell and show at the same time. Choose simple graphics or images (and try to show only one image or graphic per slide unless you need to show a side-by-side comparison).

4. **Use ≤ six bullets per slide:** This corollary to the content principle of using ≤ six words per bullet point means, of course, that you will have at most 36 words on the slide. (Even The Text Doctor can do **that** math.) Having fewer bullet points will allow you to focus your attention, hopefully enough to force you to keep one idea per slide (bravo!). If you have more than six bullet points per slide, combine bullet points or split the slide into two or more slides.

5. **Edit visually:**  To do this, step back and look at your slide visually as if through your readers' or participants' eyes. Work hard to ensure that your text and visuals work together and that you have balanced consistency with variety. To gain variety in your slides, feel free to change your format slightly every four slides or so.

## Navigation tips

Recently, I sat through an economics professor's live slide presentation on capitalism versus democratic socialism and watched him violate every presentation principle that I pose above. But what was worse was that he had no idea how to advance his own slides and had to have someone in the audience do that for him.

In a webinar, your audience will not see you struggle in person as we saw that professor struggle, but if you learn a few easy PowerPoint tricks, you will present your webinar slides much more professionally.[1]

---

[1] Although PowerPoint is not the only presentation software available, enough people use it that I think these tips are worth passing on. And if you use different presentation software, you may find that it supports the same or similar capabilities.

Here are some PowerPoint navigation and keyboard shortcuts[2] to enhance your navigation:

- Use a remote to advance your slides or to return to the previous slide in your webinar. If you don't have a remote:
  - Press the letter P while in slide view to navigate instantly to the previous slide and N to go to the next slide.
  - Use the front and back keys on the keyboard to move forward and backward in your slides. However, be cautious – I have made mistakes that way by hitting the wrong key.
  - Jump to a slide that is not adjacent to your current slide by simply typing in the number of the slide (say, 32) and pressing ENTER. Surprise! Automagically, you'll be showing slide 32. Of course, you need to remember the slide that you were on before you performed this little magic trick so that you can return to that original slide without whiplashing your viewers through your whole presentation.

If you have two monitors, use presenter view in your webinars so that you can see the following information on your second screen (see Figure 10.1):

- Actual slide
- Your slide notes, which you can use as your script
- Slide X of Y (here, Slide 9 of 109)
- Elapsed time since you launched presenter view (here, 00:07)
- The current time (here, 1:25 PM)
- A ribbon of the last slide, current slide, and next five+/- slides

---

[2] https://support.office.com/en-us/article/keyboard-shortcuts-for-use-while-delivering-a-presentation-in-powerpoint-2010-12f0ef03-d3f4-4901-8392-e6185d1ef8d6

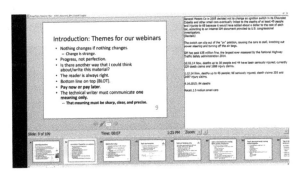

Figure 10.1 – Presenter view displays valuable information

Of course, most of the tips presented in this chapter work equally well with live presentations – you should always navigate smoothly and favor simple graphics over walls of text. The difference is that in live presentations, your personality may mitigate poor slides and questionable navigation. However, since your webinar participants usually cannot see you, your slides need to be pretty darn good.

# CHAPTER 11

# Tips for teams that produce webinars

Perhaps you work in a training department with a team that produces webinars. Or you might, like me, belong to professional organizations that offer webinars that you volunteer to produce. Sometimes, you might find yourself "voluntold" by the program chair to work on a team producing webinars for the good of your organization. I have always viewed producing webinars for my professional organizations as an opportunity to stretch myself and gain some publicity for my skills.

I've found that there are at least four roles that need to be filled when producing webinars as a team:

- Team chair
- Producer(s)
- Presenter(s)
- Participants

Table 11.1 outlines these roles and responsibilities. And you can see how these roles work in Appendix B, *Checklist for webinar teams*, which contains a list of potential individual roles within your organization or team and ideas on how you can collaborate. Realistically, one person may assume several roles, and, because every department and organization is unique, you'll want to modify and customize the checklist and the roles to meet your needs.

Table 11.1 – Roles and responsibilities needed to produce webinars

| Role | Responsibilities |
|------|------------------|
| Team chair | ■ Organizes programs for the organization, both live and by webinar<br>■ Usually manages registration and all communication with audience and presenter(s)<br>■ Appoints producer(s) and holds rehearsals |
| Producer(s) | ■ Sets up webinar in the webinar application<br>■ Assists with rehearsal(s)<br>■ Produces the webinar<br>■ Performs post-webinar production, including storing the recording |
| Presenter(s) | ■ Creates content<br>■ Delivers the presentation |
| Participants | ■ View the webinar<br>■ Chat if available<br>■ Ask and answer questions<br>■ Respond to polls if available<br>■ Take post-tests if available<br>■ Complete evaluations if available |

To go along with the table, here are some additional tips:

- Determine your individual roles as soon as you can. Once each person is comfortable with his or her role, consider trading positions in future webinars so the whole team understands the different responsibilities required. That way, if someone is absent on webinar day or leaves the organization or department, you've got the roles covered.

- After your webinar, consider holding off sending the PDF of the presenters' slides until your attendees have completed the post-webinar evaluation – a very effective quid-pro-quo.

- Debrief your team after every webinar. Debriefing lessons learned is even more important when producing as a team.

- If you find yourself participating in any of these roles and are the least bit fearful or resentful of this extra workload and learning curve, consider that you're stretching to learn a valuable technical application that may lead to further work in delivering webinars. In addition, you are helping to improve the quality of webinars in your organization or corporation.

# CHAPTER 12
# How to get going – one step at a time

Feeling overwhelmed yet? I have covered a lot of ground to help you get started delivering webinars and improving their interactivity. However, if you are still unsure about how to launch your webinar-producing career, read on.

Understanding why webinars are going to be great for you as a trainer, department, or organization will provide all the energy that you need to start the process of producing webinars. You will face a learning curve, but if you keep your motivations foremost in your mind – perhaps writing them down and reviewing them before every webinar – you will keep going until you are producing the best webinars on the planet.

Now that you have reviewed all the compelling reasons to offer webinars, here are some further steps:

- **Learn more about how webinars work:** Sign up to attend free public webinars and list what you do and don't like about their delivery and their tools. (Webinar Bucket[1] is a good source of free online events.) Aggregate that list to help you select applications and development/delivery options. Then write your goals for both selecting your webinar application and delivering your first webinar.

---

[1] http://webinarbucket.com/

- **Find a mentor:** Apprentice yourself to an experienced webinar producer, taking on more responsibilities as you get comfortable with your role. I learned almost everything I know about delivering webinars by apprenticing myself to Jane MacKenzie of Training Consultants of Sedona. I managed tasks such as handling chats, launching polls, and uploading materials to her GoToWebinar application. Eventually I felt confident enough to go out on my own.

- **Start small:** My first webinars were produced on Citrix's GoToMeeting. In that relatively simple application, I didn't have access to polling but we certainly had lively chats. I gained confidence without having too many features to master. Then I moved up to GoToWebinar, where I had polling and chat capabilities and, finally, GoToTraining, which supports polling, testing, chat, and many other interactive features. I didn't upgrade (and incur more expense) until I clearly needed more functionality, so I actually looked forward to the learning curve.

- **Continue to learn:** Read everything that you can about best practices for webinars in general. Your webinar application vendor should provide free, streaming support videos. And don't be afraid to call support for answers to questions that you cannot find on your own. Support should be delighted to help you learn new ways to use their application.

- **Strive for constant improvement:** For example, I always print out the chat logs to make sure that I answered every question, and I note those that I couldn't answer during the webinar so I can send that person an answer. I also mine chat logs to add material to my scripts in my PowerPoint Notes section. One measure of improvement for me is the length of the chat document – more chat means more interaction.

If you have learned to have fun in your live classroom, you will figure out how to have fun in your webinars. You will be able to adapt many of your classroom interactive exercises into your webinar productions. Being organized helps, simply because there is usually more technology administrivia involved in webinars than in live classroom training. We trainers are resourceful, adaptive, creative, innovative individuals who figure out hacks for problems in any training situation.

So go forth, deliver amazing webinars, and enjoy those bunny slippers!

# Bibliography

Here are a few of the resources listed in the book. I've also included some bonus references that aren't listed in the book. For a more comprehensive – and up-to-date – reference, please check out the Webliography page at: http://textdoctor.com/webinar-school-webliography.

[1] Anderson, Chris. *TED Talks: The Official TED Guide to Public Speaking.* Houghton Mifflin Harcourt. 2016. Although this book is primarily about how to present at a TED Talk, any trainer can learn a lot about passion for your topic, the need for rehearsals, using your best voice, and the future of presentations.

[2] Burton, Sharon. *8 Steps to Amazing Webinars.* XML Press. 2012. Burton addresses webinars for marketing a company's products and services.

[3] Clay, Cynthia. *Great Webinars.* Pfeiffer. 2012. Clay uses webinars to develop training, particularly in high-interaction modes such as breakout rooms and group discussions.

[4] Frick, Elizabeth. *Business Matters: A freelancer's guide to business success in any economy.* XML Press. 2013. My first book with XML Press provides guidance for freelance creatives, including trainers.

[5] Gawande, Atul. *The Checklist Manifesto: How to Get Things Right.* Metropolitan Books. 2009. Learn more about why and how checklists can be essential to every endeavor, not just webinars.

[6] Huggett, Cindy. *The Virtual Training Guidebook: How to Design, Deliver, and Implement Live Online Learning.* ASTD. 2013. Comprehensive plans and suggestions for enterprise-wide virtual learning, including webinars.

[7] Sinek, Simon. *Start with Why: How Great Leaders Inspire Everyone to Take Action.* Portfolio [The Penguin Group]. 2009. Sinek emphasizes that everyone should first explain why they do what they do before they share anything else about their presentation or training.

# Checklist for webinar trainers

- ☐ Is demographic data prepared so you can comment on where learners are located?
- ☐ Start backup computer/laptop and check for Windows update.
- ☐ Do a hard boot on your production computer/laptop.
- ☐ Log into webinar application on your production computer/laptop.
- ☐ Check that computer is connected through LAN, not wireless.
- ☐ Run speed test[1] to see current speed and troubleshoot if necessary.
- ☐ Drag production entities into place and save layout.
- ☐ Set up recording location.
- ☐ Chat (Good morning/afternoon [population]).
- ☐ Check chat location and save.
- ☐ Check on polls and open first poll (have printed polls ready).
- ☐ Check that timer is ready to launch (for activity or break).
- ☐ Have attendance sheet ready.
- ☐ Turn off or silence any devices that might make sounds.
- ☐ Pull browser to Monitor 1 (or wherever slides will show).

## 15 minutes before

- ☐ Get room temperature beverage and straw and 3 cough drops.
- ☐ Check that PowerPoint Presenter View is on the correct monitor.
- ☐ Go to first slide and pause screen.
- ☐ Show your screen.
- ☐ Plug in microphone or dial in; test sound; mute yourself.
- ☐ [Put dog elsewhere.]
- ☐ Close/lock door to office or conference room.
- ☐ Put up screen behind you as sound absorber (optional).
- ☐ Suck on a cough drop.
- ☐ Unmute and test sound again.

---

[1] http://www.speedtest.net/

## Start webinar

☐ Remove "paused."
☐ Start webinar.
☐ START RECORDING!

## BREAK

☐ Start timer, pause webinar, pause recording, mute self.
☐ Stop timer, start recording, unmute self, start webinar again.

## Close out webinar

☐ Save chat log before closing out.
☐ Close out to convert recording (if necessary).

## Post-production after closing webinar

☐ Upload recording to storage; send link to attendees if sharing recording with them.
☐ Send chat log if cleared with all attendees.
☐ Download attendance reports and store in folder.
☐ Download chat log; enlarge text; add date to every entry (globally); print out and add useful comments to slides (Notes section); store revised chat log in folder.
☐ Unmute/unsilence devices that you muted earlier.
☐ List "lessons learned" from this webinar that will help you improve the next webinar!

Assumptions: 1) You have two displays. 2) You connect to the Internet through a LAN, not wireless. 3) Your webinar application has polling and chatting functions. 4) You use Microsoft PowerPoint. 5) You have a dog.

Download a printable version of this checklist at: http://textdoctor.com/-webinar-school-webliography.

# Checklist for webinar teams

**Webinar title:** _____     **Date:** _____

| What to do | Details | Responsible party |
|---|---|---|
| **3 - 4 weeks before** | | |
| Set up webinar in your webinar application | Be sure to use keywords in the title/description | Organizer/Producer |
| Get information on website | Webinar description, registration link, and payment tool button (if needed) | Organizer/Producer |
| Write e-mail campaign | | Organizer/Producer |
| Advertise | Social media and E-mail lists | Organizer/Producer |
| Check your webinar application and payment tool | Every 2 – 3 days, through the morning of the webinar, check your webinar application for new registrations<br><br>Check your payment tool for payments<br><br>Confirm paid registrants in your webinar application if necessary | Organizer/Producer |
| **2 - 3 weeks before** | | |
| Prepare presentation with polling and chat questions | | Presenter |
| Add polling questions to your application | | Producer |

| What to do | Details | Responsible party |
|---|---|---|
| Add survey questions to your application | | Producer |
| **One week before** | | |
| Rehearse | Check functioning of polling questions<br><br>Check audio functions<br><br>Define roles/responsibilities | Presenter/Producer |
| Prepare handout | Get handout ready for distribution | Presenter |
| PR reminder | Send e-mail to organization and social media to remind of last chance to register | Organizer/Producer |
| **Day before** | | |
| Provide final handout(s) | Some presenters and organizations prefer to send handouts after the webinar (often sending only if participants complete evaluation) | Presenter |
| Print out slides | Six or more on a page, single-sided; set up numbers on slides large enough to see when printed | Presenter |
| Practice, practice, practice | Practice to know timing, avoid stumbling | |
| **Day of event** | | |
| Bring cell phone into office | Silence cell phone | Presenter/Producer |

| What to do | Details | Responsible party |
|---|---|---|
| Boot up laptop; reduce screen resolution if necessary | | Presenter/Producer |
| **Immediately prior to event** | | |
| Sign onto your webinar application 30 minutes prior to event | | Presenter/Producer |
| Call into your webinar application or start using VOIP | Before dialing on landline: press *70 to avoid incoming calls; all goes to VM. | Presenter/Producer |
| Open presentation | | Presenter |
| Test audio equipment | | Presenter/Producer |
| Set up recording location | | Presenter |
| Expand chat and poll and audience view and set chat log location | | Producer |
| Start screen sharing | One minute prior to broadcast | Presenter |
| **To start event** | | |
| Click Start | | Presenter |
| Click Start Recording | | Presenter |
| Click to second slide | | Presenter |
| **During event** | | |
| Start webinar/introduction | | Presenter |

| What to do | Details | Responsible party |
|---|---|---|
| Respond to technical questions | | Producer |
| Respond to content questions | | Presenter |
| Post polling questions | Post questions<br><br>Monitor response verbally<br><br>Announce when you're closing the poll | Producer |
| Monitor time/progress | | Presenter/Producer |
| If opening phone lines, monitor question hands (if available) | | Producer/Presenter |
| Call on participants to ask questions by chat or raising hands (if available) | Note: Producer can send chat to Presenter to guide to a particular participant.<br><br>Or, have producer monitor sequence of hands and tell presenter who was first. | Presenter |
| Open participant line | | Producer |
| Call on next participant | | Presenter |
| Close first phone line | | Producer |
| Open second phone line | | Producer |
| Use timer for break | CLOSE TIMER AFTER BREAK | Producer/presenter |
| Bring webinar to close, based on time or absence of questions | | Presenter |

| What to do | Details | Responsible party |
|---|---|---|
| Set up location to save chat log (unless you've done it earlier) | | Presenter/Producer |
| Set up question-saving location if available | | Presenter/Producer |
| Shut down the webinar application | | Presenter/Producer |
| **After event** | | |
| Download recording | | Presenter |
| Check recording | | Producer/Presenter |
| Send recording to those requesting it | Anyone who registers and pays but cannot attend automatically receives the recording stored on your choice of storage application | Producer |
| Follow up to questions/comments from survey or attendance report | | Presenter |
| Set up recording on website shopping cart if you're selling the recording | | Presenter |

Download a printable version of this checklist at: http://textdoctor.com/-webinar-school-webliography.

# Image Credits

The cover image and the XML Press logo are copyright © XML Press. The introductory images at the top of the bibliography and chapters 1, 2, 3, 4, 5, 6, 7, 8, 9, and 11 are licensed from iStock.[1] Except as noted below, all other images are copyright © Elizabeth Frick.

### Chapter 1, *Webinar training compared to live classroom training*

- Bunny slippers image is licensed from iStock.

### Chapter 4, *Producing and presenting your live training webinar*

- Clock image from Pixabay,[2] CC0 Public Domain[3]
- Figure 4.1 is licensed from iStock.

### Chapter 6, *Low-tech tips for interactivity*

- Figure 6.2 copyright © CC by SA 3.0, Wikipedia commons user Topjur01.[4]

### Chapter 9, *Expect three surprises!*

- Figure 9.1 US Government, Public Domain. Taken by Photographer's Mate 2nd Class Saul McSween, US Navy.

### Chapter 12, *How to get going – one step at a time*

- Introductory image copyright © Konstantinos Mavroudis, CC by SA 2.0.[5]

---

[1] http://istockphoto.com
[2] https://pixabay.com
[3] https://creativecommons.org/publicdomain/zero/1.0/deed.en
[4] https://creativecommons.org/licenses/by-sa/3.0/
[5] https://creativecommons.org/licenses/by-sa/2.0/

# Index

# Colophon

## About the Author

Dr. Elizabeth (Bette) Frick teaches writing and communication by webinar to learners all over the world. Bette holds a PhD in English from the University of Minnesota and served as president of the Twin Cities chapter of the Society for Technical Communication (STC) from 2003–2004. She is a Fellow of the STC.

Dr. Frick is also board-certified as a medical editor by the Board of Editors in the Life Sciences (BELS) and serves as the Immediate Past President of the American Medical Writers Association Rocky Mountain Chapter (AMWA-RMC). She is the author of *Business Matters: A freelancer's guide to business success in any economy,* also published by XML Press.

## About XML Press

XML Press (http://xmlpress.net) was founded in 2008 to publish content that helps technical communicators be more effective. Our publications support managers, social media practitioners, technical communicators, and content strategists and the engineers who support their efforts.

Our publications are available through most retailers, and discounted pricing is available for volume purchases for business, educational, or promotional use. For more information, send email to orders@xmlpress.net or call us at (970) 231-3624.